TABLE OF CONTENTS

"Great security starts with an understanding of risk"

"Great security starts with an understanding of risk"

Preface

This book is written from the views and experience of Kevin L. Mabry, in the field of Data Security. I have seen many different aspects of data breaches, some small some large. One of the most alarming thing I've seen is the difference between how enterprise companies and small businesses view and value their data. Large enterprises, 1,500 employees and above, view data security as just a part of doing business and is fully willing to budget and spend the money to protect one of their most valued assets, their data. While on the other hand small businesses view data security as just

3

"Great security starts with an understanding of risk"

another "THING" that wants to take their money, and they choose not to invest in protecting their data. In my experience I have even come across some small business owners that believe that Ransomware or even hackers, just aren't real and they couldn't believe that someone would really do that, "BELIEVE IT"!

That is why I'm writing this book, to debunk the thinking of the small business owner relating to Data Security and hopefully open their eyes to the truth. One of the main reasons that statistics are so bad about data breaches and ransomware is because of the practices of smaller businesses. Just picking on one stat, "the average data breach goes undetected for

"Great security starts with an understanding of risk"

more than 200 days", the main reason it is over

200 days is because these surveys are adding

small businesses in with the statistics. For

instance, the Target breach went undetected for

20 days, while a small 10-person law firm was

breached for over 274 days. This is just one

example, there are many more. As you can see

Target, large enterprise, 20 days, small 10-

person law firm, 274 days.

The whole premise around this book is to

help small business owners understand that

they have a duty to protect this data they hold,

use, transmit, whatever they do with it, it needs

to be guarded with the same enthusiasm that

large enterprises protect theirs. I hear of small

"Great security starts with an understanding of risk"

businesses shutting down just because they didn't do the "RIGHT" thing and protect the data that was entrusted to them and it came back to bite them. In the United States, small businesses make up over 92% of all businesses, so that means collectively they hold the majority of all the data out there. So yes, they have a HUGE responsibility to their customers, families, the country, and lastly the fate of their own business do step up their game relating to Data Security. Fellow business owners, this book is not being written to scare you but to open your eyes, that Data Security is not just about large companies, but it is about all companies no matter the size and we all have something

"Great security starts with an understanding of risk"

hackers want. Don't ignore these warnings, but heed them and make the first step.

I would like to first and foremost thank God almighty for the ability to gain the knowledge I have and share it with you. He also blessed me with an awesome wife Cathy Mabry, who has been by my side this whole journey and 3 beautiful daughters, I am truly the most blessed man in the world!

"Great security starts with an understanding of risk"

This is a snapshot of my time spent studying and evaluating why small business are having such a hard time with managing their #1 Risk, Data Security! More importantly this book reveals both the opportunities and the dangers your company will face if you are COMPLACENT in your Security practices.

Up till now True Data Security has been closely held and only available to large fortune 500 companies. For years these enterprise corporations have retained highly-trained security teams to assist in understanding the risks and necessary risk-mitigation strategies to compete in a global market.

Well known organizations including Visa International, Bank of America, and American Express have paid upwards of $200,000/yr. per engineer and have contracted with leading security firms at fees ranging from $100,000 to $150,000 quarterly to have outside experts assess and uncover risks associated with the technologies that are address in this report. But this is NOT about large enterprises. It's about YOU and your journey into what we are calling, "THE DIGITAL REVOLUTION."

"Great security starts with an understanding of risk"

We will uncover an IDEA which will allow you to safely leverage the same transformational technologies used by The F500 (Fortune 500 Corporations) to 10X your business this year. You can now enter the digital revolution without exposing your all of your ideas and money to threats (which will destroy you) if you understand the hidden truths I am about to disclose.

Who Am I And Why You Should Listen To Me

My name is Kevin L. Mabry, CEO of Sentree Systems, Corp. We specialize in helping small businesses mitigate and manage RISK and have been doing this since 1999. I have appeared on local evening news channels to discuss current breaches and how they affect the local community. I have also written an article in the Indiana CPA Society 2016 fall publication. I sit on the advisory board to a non-profit organization which helps families stay connected. I am also on a local Cybersecurity Council. I recently became a member of Indiana's FBI Infraguard cybersecurity program,

"Great security starts with an understanding of risk"

which is a great platform for sharing data breach information.

To help you understand why I'm so passionate about this topic, let me share with you just ONE cybercrime horror story...In fact, let me share with you a personal story about my own brush with cybercrime that may help you understand why I'm so passionate about this.

...My Own Personal Cyber Security Nightmare

Many years ago I was just like most business owners, just trying to make it with minimal support and little money. I had a MagicJack phone for my business line and it was having issues, so I did like everyone else I Googled it. Now at that time I didn't really take Security very seriously so I didn't even have an Anti-virus on my computer. I contacted the first MagicJack support number that I saw online. Little did I know this was not MagicJack it was a Social Engineer seeking to gain access to my computer to leak as much data as possible. They asked if they could log in to see if they could find the issue, so I let them. Next thing you know I saw just random lines of code running up and down my screen and I saw documents trying to open that had nothing to do with my phone. They started asking me for my mother's maiden name, which also had nothing to do with my phone. I asked them why you need that. They just told me it is just for verification. I immediately hung up the phone and disconnected my computer

10

from the internet. This situation left me feeling so VIOLATED, that someone had forced their way into my system, where I have pictures of my family, where I have my banking information and so much other personal items. I HAD to do something!

Later I had talked to a friend of mine and he told me the same thing happened to his wife, but she went even further with them and they were afraid to use their computer. They decided to get another computer and I told them I did the same thing. You never know just what they put on your computer when something like that happens.

That incident made me want to do something. I was SO ANGRY that this happened to me and another family and I know we aren't the only ones! It was unbelievable! They are hardworking business owners just like you and me. We didn't deserve to be attacked by these criminals that are too afraid to show their face that they hide behind a computer screen. That's why I decided to start a personal mission to help – and at least EDUCATE – as many business owners as I could about the dangers of cybercrime and how they can protect themselves from losing everything.

"Great security starts with an understanding of risk"

Joining The Digital Revolution

Driven by the demand for speed, flexibility, agility, and anywhere-access, your consumers have fully embraced a connected world. Look at Amazon. Amazon is so successful people are paying a $99 membership fee before they even start shopping!!!!!!!! Over the past few years they've announced 2-day delivery and are testing one hour delivery by drones and self-driving trucks.

Amazon's vision is to sell everything. They sell just about any product you would find in a mall or Walmart. They host their member's music and video libraries, automatically restock consumables, provide 2-Day free shipping (under the Prime Membership), and even offer low cost storage options to both large and small businesses. Amazon is just one example of what is to come when the right technology is applied.

Then there is Uber. Uber offers another great example. Uber has taken our country by storm. Their future is built on robotics – self-driving cars. If you've taken Uber, you know it's faster, cheaper, and more efficient than any taxi

"Great security starts with an understanding of risk"

company. The best part is there's no money exchange, so it's more secure. Will taxis survive? I don't know, but the message is clear. Your customers want a different type of experience, and technology is paving the way.

Amazon, Uber, Airbnb, and mobile banking all offer examples of what millennials (and just about any future customer) will demand going forward.

Cloud technology is yet another kind of example. Cloud technology is foundational to all of these transformations. I'm sure you've heard of virtual storage and you're probably using at least one cloud app right now. Analysts estimate cloud technology sales to reach $191 billion by 2020. Gartner says cloud solutions are one of the top 10 strategic technology trends for this year.

In addition to process efficiencies and cost reductions, cloud offers scalability, time to market, and a global reach your customers have come to expect. In a recent KMPG survey, nearly 800 technology industry leaders ranked cloud as

"Great security starts with an understanding of risk"

the technology that will have the greatest impact on business transformation this year.

Big impact areas include reductions in TCO (total cost of ownership), mobility, improved customer experience, greater customer insights, better product innovation, global expansion of your business, and improved time to market.

The fact is, your business will be running on the cloud and taking advantage of these technology enablers before you know it.

If you thinking cloud is just a way to save money, think again...

Consider past hindrances to small business IT. **Now the small business (and even the micro business) can be as big as you want it to be.** And, as new high-tech innovations come to market, your business will have greater ability to respond and adapt, creating new business opportunities.

Advancements include marketing with big data, automation through robotics, product

"Great security starts with an understanding of risk"

support using IoT, and customized social networking applications which enable you to interact with suppliers and those you serve.

This digital revolution is already in motion. Businesses are, and will continue to adopt these trends at an increasing rate. IoT is everywhere. Robotics might seem out of reach but Uber and self-checkout offer everyday examples. The industrial revolution is over. Enter the DIGITAL REVOLUTION.

Overall the benefits outweigh the risks. However, before you make the move there are some things you need to know. And as you make the inevitable switch, you will want to take the necessary steps to ensure your data stays out of the hands of criminals and competitors.

The one Thing that Could SHUT Your Business DOWN

Every time I go into a new business I am shocked by how almost everybody is

"Great security starts with an understanding of risk"

approaching their business technology decisions the wrong way.

Like every utopia, there's a catch. Security.

The question you should be asking before diving into any new technology this pervasive is, "Is it secure?"

So while I agree there are many amazing benefits, security is an issue you can't ignore or even delegate. Digitalization comes with risks...

For instance, "Cloud Security" – some would say is an oxymoron. Bruce Schneier (author of Secrets and Lies) comments on cloud-based back-up solutions saying, "Cloud security is, like almost everything in technology, a trade-off:"

- Your data is far safer from irretrievable loss if it is backed up regularly to a cloud based service.
- Your data is more at risk of being stolen if it is backed up regularly to a cloud based service.

"Great security starts with an understanding of risk"

You see, it doesn't matter whether we are talking about backup solutions, hosted applications, or collaborative technologies like Dropbox or Microsoft OneDrive. ***Make NO mistake, your Internet-connected data can be accessed by a determined unauthorized user regardless of your security strategy.***

> *.....RANSOMWARE ATTACKS RISE 250 PERCENT IN 2017, HITTING U.S. HARDEST*

However, you don't need the cloud to lose your data. The truth is, data is never completely secure in any form or location. Encrypted, local, mobile, or otherwise, if data is on a network your secrets can be accessed and misused.

The Three BIGGEST Cyber Threat

Who wants your data? Three BAD GUYS (and one more I'll get to in a minute). We call them actors. These three actors represent three primary threats; cybercrime, espionage, and hacktivism. Let me explain.

17

Cybercrime Criminals Are Looking for Cash

The cybercriminal is responsible for most identity thefts you read about in the news. Credit card theft, email compromise, and healthcare information sifting are just a few examples of these financially motivated attacks. Over the past few years these attacks have grown in frequency and severity.

Yahoo recently admitted to exposing 500 million users back in 2014. Shortly after this news hit the streets, they disclosed another 1 billion accounts which were compromised. In total, *Yahoo alone is responsible for exposing over 1.5 billion user accounts!!!!*

The Bank of Bangladesh is now the victim of the world's largest bank heist in history. $800 Million Dollars were allegedly stolen through

"Great security starts with an understanding of risk"

their SWIFT system by North Korean Government sponsored hackers.

And hookup sites including Ashley Madison and AdultFriendFinder have led to 8 serious extortion attempts and even suicides, with close to 1 billion members exposed through hackers.

These attacks are not limited to big business. They are hitting small businesses in our city every day. RANSOMWARE is one more common example.

This encryption attack sneaks in undetected, making your company's data inaccessible and unusable. Ransomware quickly turns transformational technology into useless technology. Once installed, the hacker demands payments that range between $500 and tens of thousands of dollars.

....if your company was HIT with RANSOMWARE today, would you pay it?

And if you did pay, what guarantees would you have???? Will the perpetrator make

"Great security starts with an understanding of risk"

good on their promise and decrypt your data???? And what's to stop these thieves from coming back for more money in a second attack?

...Hacktivists Will Shut You Down

Hacktivism presents another GRAVE DANGER. Surely Sony's recent attack has heighten the public's awareness. In this extreme case, North Korea reacted to a recent film poking fun at Kim Jung Un (North Korea's ill-tempered dictator). The results were disastrous.

Confidential emails revealed ugly brand-damaging language. Company stock prices collapsed, and the financial outlook of their production film was devastated!

Sony's only recourse was to pick up the pieces and move on. The FBI and US Government were powerless to stop these attacks or make up Sony's losses. When you're attacked it's up to you to find a way to survive.

"Great security starts with an understanding of risk"

Both defense and recovery are yours alone to figure out

Other attacks carried out by activist groups such as Lulzsec and Anonymous have dominated the headlines over the years. These attacks are politically motivated, targeting companies and groups with opposing political, social and moral beliefs. In every instance, the results have been hard-hitting.

Make no mistake, hacktivist groups wield tremendous power, often announcing the attack beforehand and bringing devastation regardless of the target-company's preparedness.

Nation-State Sponsored Attacks Seek Innovation at Your Expense

Read the news and you'll see daily occurrences of espionage originating from China, Russia, and more recently Germany. Nation-State crimes focus on government, infiltrating highly secretive intelligence.

"Great security starts with an understanding of risk"

The Office of Personnel Management (OPM) was such an attack reportedly orchestrated by China. While you might see the OPM attack as an act of war, it is what our NSA and CIA Directors term as, "Responsible intelligence gathering." In other words, every government with the capability to spy online is increasingly doing so. And then there's...

The Unsuspected Fourth Actor – Who is He????

So, who is the fourth actor? It's your internal people.

A recent Wall Street Journal study revealed over 75% of employees steal from the companies they work for. **In other words, your employees are most likely stealing from you.**

If an employee is looking for a better opportunity (or gets terminated for any reason) it is highly likely they will want to take data with them. They might be sales people taking client lists, R&D personnel leaving with research

"Great security starts with an understanding of risk"

findings, or managers taking anything to give them an edge in an upcoming interview.

You can't afford to dismiss internal threats. While I am not calling for you to distrust every employee, it is important to understand, desperate people steal. If they are deep in debt or faced with major financial pressures, an employee will do just about anything to survive. Like any large business accounting practice, auditing and shared accountability only demonstrate a company's prudence and responsibility.

What is Risk and What Does it Mean to Small Businesses

Risk is just a part of doing business and small businesses have a tough time mitigating and managing it. When it comes to risk in a small business, it's like the pile of dirt that gets swept under the rug and everyone tries to forget that it exists. Unfortunately, risk doesn't know how to just go away and leave you alone.

There are different types of risk to businesses, Strategic Risk, Compliance Risk,

"Great security starts with an understanding of risk"

Financial Risk, Operational Risks, Reputational Risk, and many others. But there is one risk that can affect all other risk a business comes across, and that is Security Risk. If your security strategy is inadequate then you can be out of compliance, which regulatory finds or court fees can haunt you for losing client data. If you are not following security best practices, you are running the risk of losing everything. If you lose client data they could tell others and report your organization to the BBB, which will cause reputation loss. I could go on, but as you can see, Security Risk Management is very serious.

How Does Security Really Work

Have you ever thought about how security works, I'm talking about all security, home security, bank security, security at an airport? Let's look at security in general. Take your house, how do you secure your home? Some of the things that we use to secure our homes are a fence, doors, windows, locks, alarms, guns, crime watch, monitoring, police, dogs and Insurance. We have been told that these things

"Great security starts with an understanding of risk"

secure our home, but these things are NOT what secures a home.

What secures a home is a system comprised of these individual components. That system is what we call, a layered security system and all three layers, Protection, Detection and Response, must work in sequence to have a true security system.

Doors	Alarm	Dog
Locks	Motion Detector	Guns
Windows	Monitoring	Police
Fence	Crime Watch	Insurance
Protection	Detection	Response

"Great security starts with an understanding of risk"

Security is a mindset, not a product and the sooner business owners understand this concept the sooner they can minimize their Risks. I'm not pointing the finger at small business owners because they were told by their IT provider that Anti-virus and Firewalls are the things that would keep them safe, nor am I blaming the IT provider because they were told by the vendors, that their new "PRODUCT (Shiny Thing)" is the best thing since sliced bread and it would take away all of the business owners concerns about security. Unfortunately, none of this is TRUE, no one has it covered, if they did why are we still having so many BREACHES? Why is the Cybercrime industry expected to be a 2 Trillion Dollar industry by 2019, why is Ransomware a growing problem? It is because unfortunately we can't stop them, and we have the wrong mindset about security all together. Our best defense is to DETECT and RESPOND.

In the image above the most important layer of security is the detection layer, you can't respond to a threat if you don't know it exists. If someone breaks in your house and you don't have an alarm, or a dog to bark, or motion detection, or anything to let you know that an

"Great security starts with an understanding of risk"

intruder has broken past your protection layer, what would be your response? What is your next step? NOTHING, you have no respond because you don't know they are there.

This is why security is failing for small businesses because they do not have the resources to detect nor a plan to respond. At HomeFireDrillDay.com they talk about having a plan for escape. They promote having Home Fire Drills, we need to do the same for security in our homes as well as our businesses. This is what large fortune 500 companies do, they have their plans written out and they practice them, over and over. They assign a security officer, someone to call on when there is an issue, and that person creates a team to support their mission. In fortune 500 companies, they have the resources to hire full time personnel for these positions, but for a small business, this would be one of those multi-job positions. You may have the receptionist or office manager be the security officer and have the shipping personnel be their backup.

"Great security starts with an understanding of risk"

Why Traditional Network Security Doesn't Work

When I started Sentree Systems in 1999, we were a generalist IT company just like all the rest. We focused on all things productivity, what it took to keep my clients up and running smooth as possible with minimal downtime. We offered everything technology based because we wanted to make it easy for our clients so they didn't have to go to multiple vendors for technology we could provide.

In 2012 I started seeing and hearing about security breaches being on the rise, but it was all about large enterprises and some large mid-size businesses. I was lead to believe that hackers and cyber criminals where only attacking larger organization, but boy was I WRONG. I soon learned that they had been turning their eyes towards small businesses, but I saw the same old stuff coming from the IT companies. They still were focused on "Productivity" not security. I saw this as a huge problem and it needed to be addressed soon because it was just going to get worse, and it has. Year over year since that time

"Great security starts with an understanding of risk"

breaches have been increasing over 100's of percentages and that is NOT COOL!

Around the same time as my MagicJack problem, I set out on a quest to investigate the reason why we as a country are having such a huge issue with security. I quickly learned that it was my fault, well IT's fault when it comes to small businesses. Small businesses have been relying on IT generalist for years because that is the cheapest way to go. Yes, IT knows about security, but trust me they are not security specialist and if you want to STOP the bleeding you need someone or an IT company that has a security specialist on staff. I learned that IT has been following their vendor's recommendations for security and I understand that the vendor's job is to sell their product. As the owner of a small business you need to take the security officer roll because security is not an IT issue it is a business risk issue and that affects your bottom line.

I followed this story for the next couple of years and I switched my company to a Security Consulting Agency. Our main focus is on security, what that means is that if you need a server installed you are going to get the most

"Great security starts with an understanding of risk"

secured server, not just a server that "SERVES". We do not sell you the next best ANTI-VIRUS product that comes out because that may not be what you need. We base all decisions on your unique business and your unique needs, because no two businesses are exactly the same. You may already have a good enough anti-virus so why should you upgrade. But, if you don't have a detection solution, that is where we will place our focus.

What About Small Businesses? Is Your Business Vulnerable?

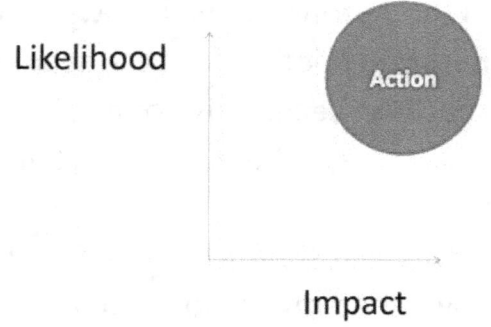

Small business has become a major target for hackers. It's the big companies that

"Great security starts with an understanding of risk"

dominate national media, but small businesses are losing every day. And transformational technologies are only making data loss easier. To understand how data theft is happening, let's take a look at now cyber criminals are getting in.

What's the one thing every business leader should understand? I refer to it as The Impact vs. Likelihood Chart. I did not come up with this, I learned it from David Stelzl a great CISSP that has been instrumental in my Security training and studies. Every business leader owns digital assets and that means you. Some of your assets are worth everything to your company.

The impact vs. likelihood chart explains how you should view and assess data and the risk of losing your most important digital assets.

In a book, written by David Stelzl called Digital Money, he explains how your data is a currency. Data is an asset which is being created and transmitted by every computer device in your office. Your secrets and customer information might be in the cloud or on a smartphone or tablet. Chances are these assets are associated with an application you use to conduct business.

"Great security starts with an understanding of risk"

The X-Axis of the impact vs. likelihood chart provides a quantitative measure of impact associated with these assets. On the Y-Axis is a measurement of likelihood.

The question you should be asking is, "What are the odds we will suffer the impact of a disaster?" Next ask, "Is our risk trending up or down? Is it growing or shrinking? And how are we managing it?"

Security is more a people problem than it is a technical one. Many of the losses you read about could be prevented if people better understood how security works. In fact there is one major mistake I see just about every business making when it comes to securing digital assets. Before we uncover this important concepts there are 7 key areas of threat you need to know about as you consider the use of transformational technologies to grow your business.

7 Major Threats That Will Take You Down

Following are 7 things you should be watching for over the next 12 months. In each of these concerns you will see a technical issue. But, underlying most are people problems.

"Great security starts with an understanding of risk"

Let's take a look...

1. **False Since of Security.** First, it's important to understand (regardless of what you've been told) firewalls and passwords don't keep hackers out. If your data is on a network or in the cloud, it is accessible to a hacker no matter what you do.

This may sound like a hopeless situation but as I will show you later in this book, there are things you can do to greatly minimize your risk. And if you bring your risk down to an acceptable level you can continue to leverage the technologies I've already mentioned without too much worry. As I've already stated, the benefits outweigh the risks when technology is approached correctly.

2. **Social Engineering.** You've probably heard the term social engineering. It's not new. But don't underestimate the power the hacker has through social engineering attacks.

Almost every major attack involves social engineering. Social engineering is used to con unaware users into installing programs on their computers which in turn give access to the hacker. Examples targeting small businesses like

"Great security starts with an understanding of risk"

yours include CATO (Corporate Account Takeover) and Invoice Fraud Redirect.

In the case of CATO, hackers take over your email and begin issuing orders to carry out directives only you are authorized to perform. A common ruse is to email your accounts payable person requesting a wire transfer to a supplier or customer.

In a recent case, one small business owner transferred over $400,000 to three suppliers which should not have been paid. Of course, the wire transfer information directed these funds to the hacker's account. The victim's $400,000 is not recoverable. And per bank policy, while individuals have 60 days to report fraudulent activities, in most cases you only have 24 hours as a small business owner.

3. **Mobility and BYOD (Bring Your Own Device).** BYOD initiatives are going on in companies all over our city right now. Since almost every aspect of life involves technology, drawing a hard line between work and personal life is becoming impossible.

The danger comes in thinking computing on one device or in one location is just as safe as

"Great security starts with an understanding of risk"

another. And so, your employees are likely to treat your most sensitive data as they would their personal email or media collection. They will store and transmit your company's secrets just about anywhere and on any device. The employee's assumption is, security technology has me covered. They're wrong.

4. **Misuse of Social Media.** The use of social media at work is an ongoing Achilles Feel for office managers. Facebook and Instagram are time wasters. But wasting time is of little concern when compared to the mindset social media has created.

Remember when people were afraid to purchase online? Or when you were scared to write something about yourself or post a family photo? That's gone. People send naked pictures of themselves across the Internet every day. If they're willing to expose themselves, what will they do with your data?

In a recent WSJ article, one financial firm reported 73% of the men in their company giving up highly sensitive information to a woman on Facebook. But get this, 13% of these trusted-workers gave away company passwords. You might have guessed this "woman" was a 40-

"Great security starts with an understanding of risk"

year-old male, white hat hacker, posing as a woman to test the integrity of the firm's office workers. How can companies like yours protect against such irresponsible behavior?

5. **Internal Threats.** Cybercriminals, spies, and hacktivists are real. But in just about every major data breach, there's an internal component. In some cases its operator error. In other cases, it's a bribe to cooperate with an outsider.

The perimeter security mindset assumes the threat is always outside, yet as I have already pointed out, employees admit they steal data. When employees are laid off, don't get promoted, or move on to a better opportunity, you can assume they'll be taking data with them. But it's also true that a hacker can easily bribe one of your employees, giving them 5 to 10 times what they make in salary, to cooperate in a data heist.

6. **Nation-State & Advanced Persistent Threats.** You've may seen the term "Advanced Persistent Threat," or APT. What is it? APTs are groups of people that want in – they are a "who", not a "what".

"Great security starts with an understanding of risk"

Google "Stuxnet" (a highly sophisticated attack targeting the Iranian nuclear uranium enrichment program) and you'll get a glimpse of the power hackers have over us. Or consider cyberwarfare attacks that have taken down power grids – they're seemingly unstoppable.

The APT is bigger than malware. These groups are sophisticated, well sponsored by Nation-States, and determined to get something they specifically want. In other words, they are "Persistent."

7. **Cyberterrorism.** Finally, there is the growing threat of war or cyberterrorism.
While this is not a targeted attack on the small business owner or entrepreneur, the impact is real. In a worst-case scenario, hacker groups will take down power grids and other critical infrastructure you rely on for your business. There's not much you can do to protect yourself here. The best thing is to be aware of it, and at some level be prepared for disaster and recovery.

"Great security starts with an understanding of risk"

Misunderstanding compliance can kill your company!

Compliance is not security. Lawmakers would like you to think HIPAA (Healthcare privacy requirements) GLBA (the Banks equivalent of HIPAA), and PCI (Credit Card Industry Requirements) compliance will keep your data safe. They won't.

The undisclosed truth is, compliant companies get hacked all the time. Compliance rules are set up to move a company toward security, but in no way are these cumbersome regulations actually addressing the problem. The problem is, compliance falls short. According to Mike McConnell, former Director of National Security to the White House is, "Once a company passes the compliance audit, they stop working on security." Compliance is the law, but in my opinion it's too often just a distraction from true security.

Are You The Hacker's Target?

In a recent WSJ article we were told small businesses are held personally responsible for

"Great security starts with an understanding of risk"

financial losses caused by hackers. While an individual can usually recover from a fraudulent wire transfer, banks are rarely held responsible for small business losses. Small businesses have big risks.

Consider these small business statistics from The Wall Street Journal:

> ➤ "The proportion of attacks explicitly focused on small/medium business (SMB) rose to more than 30%..."

> ➤ "The total number of targeted attacks on small business organizations rose to an average of 151/day..."

Is security a priority in your business? Consider your laptops, smartphones, and 16 tablets. Firewalls are important, but much of your data is outside the firewall, exposed through email, insecure websites, and mobile devices. How secure is your business?

"Great security starts with an understanding of risk"

Is Your Company in Danger of Becoming a Statistic...?

Statistical Data from the Wall Street Journal

➢ 77% of SMBs say their company is safe from cyber-threats, such as hackers, viruses, malware or a cybersecurity breach.

➢ 88% of SMB companies have no formal cyber security plan in place today.

➢ 73% of respondents said a safe and trusted Internet is critical to their success.

➢ 59% admit they do not have a contingency plan outlining procedures for responding and reporting data breach losses (Which makes you wonder about the 73% cited above).

➢ 66% stated they are not concerned about cyber-threats (external or internal), such as an employee, ex-employee, or contractor or consultant stealing data...(even though the WSJ reported last

"Great security starts with an understanding of risk"

year that 75% of employees admit they steal company data!)

➤ 86% said they are satisfied with the amount of security they have in place to protect customer or employee data.

➤ 83% said they "strongly or somewhat agree" they are doing enough or making enough investments to protect customer data.

Notice the inconsistencies. In another recent report, Visa found that small business represented more than 90% of the reported credit card breaches, and Symantec found almost 40% of the more than 1 billion cyber-attacks in a three-month period, targeted companies with **less than 500 employees!** Small business is a target.

Hackers know that innovation comes from small businesses. It's a well-known fact smaller companies like yours are coming up with the great entrepreneurial ideas. The larger companies then buy smaller companies to gain access to innovation.

"Great security starts with an understanding of risk"

It is also well known that small businesses have access to bank loans and funding sources which are easily taken advantage of. Since most small businesses will never achieve the security standards found in enterprise corporations, gaining access to account numbers, wire transfers, and innovation is much easier for the hacker.

Do You Know What Your Data is Worth?

Data is the new GOLD. People want this digital form of currency and will do all kinds of unethical things to get it. In most cases these attacks are not personal. Theft is a result of desperate people grabbing what they can to meet their needs at your expense.

But these attacks are not always targeted. That means the criminal doesn't need to know your name or where you live. Their tools are stealth and far reaching. We call these class attacks. Class attacks are sent out across the Internet, landing on exposed computing devices

"Great security starts with an understanding of risk"

which store and process your most valuable assets. Some will take your data, some will scam you out of money, and others will destroy your reputation through extortion or exposure. Let's take a look at what you're up against.

Data Loss & Privacy – Are You Exposed?

Where is your data stored? Who has access to it? What laws govern it? These are all issues companies like yours have never had to deal with until cloud and Internet.

Privacy online is a challenge. Since the cloud and Internet are global they span every region of the world. Depending on where your data is in this massive mesh of connected systems, the laws will vary.

Take note, using cloud services from providers outside the US may change the way your data is governed. Privacy laws can be complicated and problematic for a business like yours to fully comprehend. For instance, in countries such as Germany, you might be subject to prosecution for allowing a bit of personal data to leave the country or be viewed

"Great security starts with an understanding of risk"

inappropriately. Businesses in Europe often require their data be stored in country, protected by local laws. That's not the case in the US. And what about India, where many technology providers are turning for lower cost infrastructure and labor options? How is your data treated under India's laws?

When data is stored locally in your office you have complete control over how and where your data is used. You control the access and privacy. Introducing cloud applications changes everything. You no longer know where your data is stored or who has access rights. You can't even guarantee it is encrypted.

And then there's data aggregation. Everything you do today is being recorded digitally, greatly reducing your privacy. There are four global data aggregators in the world today which are buying up data to profile you and me. Your data in the hands of the wrong people can bring disaster.

The bottom line is, when people (including criminals) gain access to your data they gain the power to impersonate you. Put this power in the hands of a scammer and you may find yourself victimized by all kinds of horrors including

"Great security starts with an understanding of risk"

fraudulent loans, money transfers, and communications that will ruin your personal brand and reputation.

Your Intellectual Property – It's the Lifeblood of Your Business

Internet, cloud, and any connected application will put your Intellectual Property (IP) at risk. In all cases you are entrusting sensitive data to cloud and application providers. And they probably won't value it as highly as you do. Yet, you have little choice if you plan to grow your business. And then there's smartphones and tablets...

The proliferation of mobility, BYOD (Bring your Own Device), and cloud applications, further expose you as your employees create and use your data irresponsibly. Some exposures will be operator error or sheer ignorance. Other exposures will come through determined financial desperation and outright criminal intent. At times the lines will be blurred.

Understanding where your data is, who has access to it, and how it's being used is suddenly complicated. Transformational

"Great security starts with an understanding of risk"

technologies such as those I've already listed are highly distributed and highly virtualized.

There will be numerous copies of your data across virtual storage devices around the world, so how will you know every instance of your data is gone when you hit "DELETE"? Next generation computing means your most valuable secrets will be everywhere, protected by thinly secured firewalls and passwords. It's up to you to make sure cloud application providers and your own end-users handle data responsibly and securely.

Unfortunately, most business owners are more concerned with saving money. They don't realize the tremendous impact of losing data until it's too late.

Who has Control of Your Data?

There are three pillars to data security and we call it CIA, which stands for Confidentiality, Integrity, and Availability. These three pillars are all about having control of your data. Confidentiality is about preventing the wrong person from reading data they are not

"Great security starts with an understanding of risk"

authorized to read. Integrity deals with stopping and controlling the modification of data. Availability is all about having access to your data, if you don't have access, who does

Think about RANSOMWARE, if your data gets encrypted you no longer have control of your data. Not only that the have modified it without authorization. Ransomware breaks at least two of the pillars of data security Integrity and Availability. One good thing is at least they can't read it unless they siphon it from your network. OCR (Office of Civil Rights, HIPAA Compliance Agency) has declared a ransomware attack as a HIPAA breach and must be handled as one.

Three Questions You Should Constantly Be Asking Yourself

Question 1: What are your most important data assets? Start by looking at your
data. You have more than you think. Some of it resides on servers, some on laptops. Many of your company secrets are likely in email or on someone's mobile device.

"Great security starts with an understanding of risk"

Hopefully your data is backed up regularly. Where are those backups right now? What applications do you rely on most? How long can you do without them? Look at the impact of losing any one and prioritize. Next, ask...

Question 2: Who would want your data, and how would they get it? This is not just about theft. Expand your question to consider anything which might make applications or data inaccessible to your business or corrupt and unusable.

If your business is going through a layoff or legal battle, your threats look different than if you are not. A merger or acquisition would also change your threats, so look both at the value of data and the changing business climate.

You will also want to consider single points of failure or potential bottlenecks. Finally, you will want to consider your preparedness...

Question 3: Would you know in time to stop a data breach or outage? Every business leaders MUST know if they can stop a cyber-disaster before it's too late. Can you

"Great security starts with an understanding of risk"

detect it and stop it in time? How confident are you?

In summary, you need to know the top threats, the impact associated with each threat, and the likelihood something bad will happen in the near future. Then, if or when the unthinkable does happen, you must be able to detect it and stop it before business-crippling bad actors take down you and your company.

Who is Responsible for Your Security Strategy?

Answering the three questions above before implementing next generation technologies will allow you to assess increased or decreased business risk. Risk is measured through an assessment that looks quantitatively at your impact vs. likelihood.

By comparing risks to the benefits you gain with new technology, you now have the intelligence you need to make a wise decision.

"Great security starts with an understanding of risk"

Moving to the cloud for example, is somewhat confusing. No one moves to just one cloud. In fact, you'll find that between hosted applications, mobiles apps, backup solutions, and collaboration tools, you'll have many cloud service providers.

So, it's not really a question of moving or not moving. It's more a question of what to move to the cloud, and what to keep on site.

Your plan should consider all your applications, backup and recovery strategies, and tools you will use to collaborate internally as well as with your customers. In many cases, you will be developing new applications to provide a competitive advantage through customer experience.

Your application hosting partners will provide most of your ongoing data security in the cloud, while YOU will be responsible for maintaining local security and the policies and procedures that govern your security strategy.

Your greatest weakness will likely be in how people in your office handle data, so providing a strong security awareness program can go a long way in helping employees

"Great security starts with an understanding of risk"

understand how data risks change as data is created, used, stored, archived, and deleted.

The Difference Between Data Security and Data Security That Works...

In order to be secure going forward, you need detection and response. Unfortunately, the product vendors and most IT consultants are providing confusing and misleading information. They are more interested in selling a product than securing your data.

Business leaders are asking the wrong question...

"How can I secure my data for the least amount of money?"

The answer to the above question leads to a lot of disappointment, frustration, missed opportunities, and eventually heartache. In fact, this question displays a deep level of ignorance about what makes a business successful. Frankly, the question borders on absurd.

"Great security starts with an understanding of risk"

First off, it's the wrong question because the cheapest security solution is almost never reliable, or the quickest, or even effective. When all is said and done, the old saying, "You get what you pay for," rings true. And since we've already established that your data is your currency and the most valuable asset in your business' possession, when you go on without securing it you waste time and money, potentially exposing your business to ruin.

David Stelzl told me of a story about several years ago where he began addressing small business leaders through intimate round table gatherings around the country. His talks focused on the difference between real security and what everyone else out there is doing. Poling his audiences several times each month, he said he was surprised at the number of business owners were truly believed they could keep hackers out with just firewalls.

None of these firms have the ability to see inside their systems and networks. Few to none are actually assessing their risk. Almost no one knows what their true risk is.

Bottom line, "True security is the ability to detect a problem and respond to it before the

"Great security starts with an understanding of risk"

impact is realized." As you'll discover in my research, you can't keep the hacker out. You can only provide faster detection to stop these stealthy invaders as they enter.

What is the Right Question to Asking About Security

When you ask the question, **"What is the cheapest security solution we can purchase?"** you are taking a compliance-focused approach. Your focus is on getting the activity done or the checkbox checked.

The question you should be asking is about risk. **"What are our most important assets, where are they and who has access?"** You should be asking "IMPACT" questions like, "How much downtime can we afford?" "How much data can we afford to lose?" And "Who would want our data?" Don't assume the answer is, "Nobody."

Remember your data is a currency and the right hacker can turn digital assets into cash on the black market.

"Great security starts with an understanding of risk"

Having the Right Security Mindset is Key

"The bad news is, even if you build your security right, you can still be attacked and Lose".

My experience has shown me that having a deficient defense against cybercriminals (Internal and External), Nation-State Hackers, and Hacktivists can easily put your company in jeopardy of a data breach.

The key to planning successful security measures is in understanding your risk. That risk will change over time as your company grows, innovates, or competes on big deals. You may also find your political and religious positions create greater exposure to activists looking to make a statement.

The impact vs. likelihood chart is the best place to start and that means conducting a thorough assessment of risk as I've already described.

Remember, each business is different. Your products and services, types of data, online exposure, and target customer or competition make your risk exposure unique to you. Once known, you can now figure out how much to

"Great security starts with an understanding of risk"

invest in adequately securing it. In other words, you can't completely secure your company, but you can bring down your likelihood to an acceptable level of risk.

Adding the right levels of detection and an on-call response team can get you most of the way there.

It's surprising to me that I never hear anyone else in the IT Services Industry talking about these distinctions (between keeping hackers out and, detecting them and stopping them.) Only from our top security advisors at fortune 500 enterprises and large government agencies do I hear this kind of thinking.

Being an IT Services provider is about developing, installing, and continually improving the small business owner's options to secure and maintain computer systems. Your success is my mission, and your security is my passion.

As I mentioned earlier, security on your computer network is like security in your house. You can lock your doors and windows, and even add fencing. But the intruder can always get in.

"Great security starts with an understanding of risk"

You may have an alarm and perhaps monitoring detection through services like ADT, but even great detection services will not stop the criminal from getting in your home. It may deter them, but it won't keep them out. The final step in the security system is a response plan.

Your plan might include police involvement, trained dogs, or even your own personal firearms or a golf club you keep by your night stand. The point is, you'll need some protection (Layer 1), a fair amount of detection (Layer 2), and some type of response (Layer 3) to stop the intruder.

Detection/Response is the True Next-gen security Model

In the computer world, most IT companies and IT vendors have missed this truth. The security product manufacturers have told us they keep computers safe using firewalls and anti-virus software. This strategy has failed and is evidenced daily in the media. Companies are losing this battle. If you want to secure your business, you need a measurement of risk and a

56

strategy to detect and respond in real-time to an intrusion.

You're Almost Ready to Enter the Digital Revolution

The Cloud is here. Digital business is here. This is the digital revolution. If you want to compete and grow...if you want to provide premier customer service and attract brand loyalty, the only option is to get onboard.

If you're like most small businesses, you are already involved with cloud, mobility, and social media.

Over the next five years more and more of your applications will go to cloud services. Your backups will be cloud-based, and you will interact internally and with your prospects and customers through social media and online applications. You may even be making drone deliveries and using self-driving cars in the not-too-distant future.

The question is, who has control of your data?

"Great security starts with an understanding of risk"

The large enterprise companies are building in-house capabilities to constantly assess and maintain their security and risk. But the small business cannot afford the cost of building these disciplines.

Instead, small business will turn to outside technology providers to do it for them. The steps I have provided here are designed to assist you in managing your security program as you move further into the digital age.

Just like you look to your legal counsel, accountant, and perhaps a healthcare or investment advisor, you're going to need a technology advisor who understands cloud, digitalization, and security.

You can save money using next generation transformational technologies, but like any key area in your business, you'll need someone to guide you through the process of choosing wisely and overseeing these functional areas.

Digitalization will be central to the future growth of your business. This means rethinking security. Policies undergird the security of your company, but they don't stop hackers.

"Great security starts with an understanding of risk"

Compliance is necessary to avoid fines and customer issues, but it too, is not security.

Security means establishing clear policies, educating both employees and contractors on what is and is not allowed, and why. Then, putting in systems that detect policy violations resulting from error or mal-intent. Finally, you'll need a well-documented enforcement plan.

Every business owner should understand, it is impossible to prevent hackers from getting in, as well as it is impossible to completely prevent employees from taking data out.

But like accounting, a well-established auditing system, with separation of duties, makes it difficult for people to carry out any long-term theft scheme. Using reputable cloud service providers who manage these things from their side will simplify the process.

"As a business leader, it is your responsibility to know what data matters. You need to know where that data is created, what it's worth, and where it sits inside your company or with third-party organizations."

"Great security starts with an understanding of risk"

You should know who wants it, and how they might go after it. In the end, you should be poised to respond, knowing someone will go after your data. But by having the right detection strategy in place, you'll be prepared to respond before damage is done. This is the future of every successful small business.

A Quick Recap of Securing Your Data in a Digital Economy

This book was written to get you thinking about your business and your data differently than ever before.

Here's a Quick Recap:

> ➢ Big opportunities await the small business that is making an intentional move into the digital revolution.

"Great security starts with an understanding of risk"

- To compete in the future, you must have a vision for global business, connected business, and real-time, premium customer experience. Transformational technologies will be your enabler.

- Security is different for transformational technologies. Traditional security strategies will leave you open and exposed to disaster.

- There are three primary actors that want your data. They are cybercriminals (Internal and External), nation-state hackers, and hacktivists.

- All data stored or transmitted on network-connected devices is accessible to a determined hacker.

- Small business is a primary target using class attacks. Hackers know you possess more innovation and less security expertise.

- Great security starts with an understanding of risk. Risk is measured through assessments that construct the impact vs. likelihood chart.

"Great security starts with an understanding of risk"

➤ Great Security is comprised of three key elements. They are PROTECTION, DETECTION, and RESPONSE. Detection and response are often the most overlooked components, yet they are the most important part of your well-designed threat mitigation strategy.

➤ Every business should assume they have either been attacked, are being attacked, or will be attacked. Fast detection and swift response are the small business owner's only defense. FBI and government compliance can't protect or restore your business.

Let me be frank. The strategies and tactics shared in this book are just the appetizers.

The main portion is my **"Cyber-Risk Analysis"** (CRA).

So, if you're ready to build a company with unlimited potential and far reaching impact, you need to measure your risks. Putting the right security in place will give you peace of mind as you move into the digital revolution.

"Great security starts with an understanding of risk"

My CRA assessment process has changed the lives of many small business owners just ike you. And I am confident it can do the same for you.

You can learn more about these strategies at ww.sentreesystems.com. There's no risk to talk with us about your business and you can stop the process any time.

But if you let us look under the hood, we'll help you discover any potential problems before they impact your business. If everything looks good, we'll tell you. However, if we discover symptoms of a growing threat, we'll help you check them out to make sure you're not exposed to catastrophic failure.

Kevin L. Mabry, CEO

Sentree Systems, Corp.

317-939-3282

mabry_kevin@sentreesystems.com

"Great security starts with an understanding of risk"

www.ingramcontent.com/pod-product-compliance
Lightning Source LLC
Chambersburg PA
CBHW071237220526
45468CB00002B/897